21 Powerful Poetic Affirmations

Based on Law of Attraction, Law of Manifestation, NLP and Life Coaching

Sakshi Gupta

Made with ❤ on the BookLeaf Publishing Platform
www.bookleafpub.in
www.bookleafpub.com

Dedication

To the Universe

To the divine source
To my Mahadev
To my awakening
To my calling
To my intuition
To my sister
To my folks
To my clients
To my readers
To myself

Preface

The purpose of this book is to make you read these positive affirmations from time to time and on daily basis. READ THEM LOUD LIKE A MANTRA OR SING IT LIKE A SONG with confidence and faith that they are actually working for you. Because they are written in such a form that they will positively affect you in all ways possible. At first, they will transform you from within and affect you mentally. Then they will be evident in your reality. They will change your thought process and start reflecting on your actions and behavior. And I am sure you want a powerful and a positive life, a new life.

Try to write them or recite them as much as you can. Try to feel them and remember them as soon as you can. Try to practice meditation, closing your eyes, focussing on your third eye area, when you actually remember them word by word. They are powerful and based on law of attraction, law of manifestation, NLP, Life Coaching and on my intuition. They will help you all.

Take care. Love and Light.

Acknowledgements

There was this gut feeling that one day I will write a book. At least one. My intuition told me so. So I did it, finally. I have to thank my intuition and psyche for this work and for this confidence that I can write something for mankind.

I have to thank my family who has seen my transition from the corporate world to the world of life coaching. They encouraged me to stay on this path and become successful.

I must not forget the humble beginnings and the initial struggles of becoming a Life Coach and later an NLP Coach.

I should include my clients who have given me an opportunity to work with them from time to time. Each session with them has led to this amazing book.

Last but not the least I want to thank the divine, my Mahadev and myself.

1. Free Yourself

I am free from attachments.
I am free from obsessions.

I am free from results.
I am free from outcomes.

I am free from desires.
I am free from obligations.
I am free from analysis.

I am free from past times.
I am free from emotions.

I am free, free and free.
I am me, me and me.

2. Finding Your Ground

I found my ground.
I found my gratefulness.

I build my empire.
I build my character.

I lay my foundation.
I create my values.

I build my life.
I establish my aura.

I polish my life skills.
I sculpt my life path.

I work on my life.
I stand on my ground.

3. Make A New Beginning

I want a new beginning.
I invite a new beginning.
I create a new beginning.
I deserve a new beginning.

I manifest a new beginning consciously.
I manifest a new beginning subconsciously.
I manifest a new beginning unconsciously.

I am grateful for this new beginning.
I am happy with this new beginning.

I am given a new start.
I am given a fresh start.
I am at square one.
I am on a clean slate.

I am at a blissful new beginning.

4. Optimistic Approach

I am optimistic.
I am positive.
I am playful.
I am cheerful.
I am hopeful.
I am thankful.

I shine my own light.
I sing my own song.

I radiate my own sunshine.
I negate my own gloominess.

I move forward positively.
I lean forward optimistically.

I am positive energy.
I am optimism.

5. Never Give Up Attitude

I never gave up.
I never give up.
I will never ever give up.
Why should I ever give up?

I am known for not giving up.
I know myself for not giving up.

I don't give up in difficult times.
I don't give up in challenging situations.
I don't give up in highs and lows.
I don't give up on my folks.

I don't give away.
I don't give in.
I don't give up.

6. Tame Your Mind

I control my thoughts and actions.
I tame my mind and steps.
I master my intellect and reactions.

I allow my left brain to be logical.
I allow my right brain to be emotional.

I win over my drifting thoughts.
I win over my day dreaming.

I have the power of my conscious mind.
I have an awareness of my subconscious mind.
I have an intuition of my unconscious mind.

I tame my wavering mind.
I tame my wavering mind.

7. Finding Your Hidden Voice

I see my inner child.
I heal my inner child.
I free my inner child.

I unlock my hidden talents.
I unlock my hidden skills.
I unlock my hidden knowledge.
I unlock my hidden purpose.
I unlock my hidden voice.

I listen to the voice of my brain.
I hear to the voice of my soul.
I hear the voice of my heart and what it unfolds.

I have a thought process.
I have a perception.
I have a reason.
I have a voice.

8. Power Up Your Communication

I strongly communicate with myself.
I firmly communicate with others.
I energetically communicate with my higher self.
I heartily communicate with my surroundings.

I listen to all forms of interpersonal communication.
I understand all forms of written communication.
I process all forms of non-verbal communication.
I perceive all forms of visual communication.
I exchange well in all forms of verbal communication.
I reflect in all forms of mass communication.

I have powers of powerful communication.

9. Being Assertive

I am firm.
I am practical.
I am intelligent.
I am critical.

I remain focused and stay relevant.
I maintain boundaries and display honesty.
I respect and value others.

I am who I am.
I feel what I feel.
I see what I see.
My needs are my needs.

I am authentic.
I am assertive.

10. Personal Freedom

I own my life.
I form my opinion.
I have my individuality.

I make my choices.
I take my decisions.

I hold all forms of freedom.
I act in all forms of freedom.
I am self-aware of my freedom.
I am responsible for my freedom.

I stand alone.
I stand for my own.
I am not afraid of being alone.
I am empowered on my own.

11. Self Love

I hold a crown of self-appreciation.
I wear a hat of self-worth.

I flaunt my self-confidence.
I flow with my conviction.
I stand in my composure.
I hold my self-assurance.

I live for self-satisfaction.
I live for self-admiration.

I have self-esteem.
I have an acceptance of myself.
I have regards for myself.
I have an affinity for myself.

I love myself.
I live with self-love.
I am love.

12. Self Care

I take care of my well-being.
I take care of my health.
I take care of my body.
I take care of my safety.
I am consuming good nutrition.
I am completing my sleep cycle.
I am maintaining my ideal body weight.

I practice gratitude.
I often meditate.
I learn new things.
I maintain hygiene.
I clean and sanitize.
I read and write.
I talk and share.
I save and thrive.

I care about myself.
I deserve care for myself.

13. Not Escaping Reality Mindset

I monitor my imagination.
I optimise my creative power.
I control my fantasy.
I enable reality checks.

I don't create unrealistic expectations of me or of others.
I do a reality check.

I don't attract any delusions.
I don't live with illusions.
I don't deal with deceptions.
I don't see any hallucinations.

I don't practice escapism.
I don't indulge in fanaticism.

I dream in reality without being lost.
I plan my reality without being daunt.

14. Finding Mental Clarity

I know my mental health is important.
I know my mental strength is important.
I know the importance of cognitive function.
I know the importance of mental clarity.

I close my eyes to visualise.
I visualise a beam of light.
I receive that beam of light.
I let it enter in my aura.
I let it flow in me.
I let it glow from me.
I practice mindfulness.
I practice yoga and meditation.
I balance my chakras.
I balance my stress.
I spend less time on screen.
I spend more time in nature.

I talk to myself for therapy.
I heal in clarity for epiphany.

15. Develop Empathy And Compassion

I just don't understand sympathy anymore.
Because I feel empathy a little more.
I empathize with others now.
I empathize with myself right now.
I am a natural giver now.
I am a genuine helper just now.
I feel more for others.
I see more of me in others.

My compassion is conscious.
My empathy is subconscious.

I connect with others through my own transformations
and awakenings.
I associate with others through my own journey and
experiences.

I evolve support to all.
I deepen love for all.

16. Finding Your Guru

I have done inner work to meet my teacher.

I am open to receive mentoring.
I am prepared to recognise my mentor.
I trust my intuition to choose my guru.
I find my coach independently.

I seek positive transformation through my guide, my guru.
I receive well deserved blessings through my teacher, my guru.
I deserve correct guidance through my mentor, my guru.
I get important solace through my coach, my guru.

I deny to follow my guru blindly.
I block any power control of my guru.

I take actions and have faith that I will become my own guide and my own guru.

17. Become An Active Listener

I don't get trapped in my own world.
I don't wear a rose coloured glass.
I don't collapse when I don't hear what I want to hear.
I don't force my opinions just because I am right.

When I hear, I collaborate.
When I listen, I relate.
When I know, I wait.
When I understand, I reflect.
When I pay attention, I paraphrase.
When I ask questions, I encourage.
When I am interested, I engage.
When I feel, I validate.
When I judge, I avoid.

I am no more a hearer.
I am now an attentive, mindful, reflective and an active listener.

18. Burn Down Negative Mindset

I see no negativity.
I feel no negativity.
I think nothing negative.
I receive nothing negative.
I believe positivity is powerful than negativity.
I accept darkness is found in negativity.
I am aware of my own negative thoughts and I turn them
into a positive light.

I don't do any over thinking that leads to negativity.
I don't run unnecessary scenarios in my head that leads
to negativity.
I don't stick to my reasoning about any situation that
leads to negativity.
I don't jump on assumptions about anything that leads to
negativity.

I don't find anything negative.
Because I burn down everything negative.

19. Self Protection

I protect others.
I protect myself too.
I preserve others.
I preserve myself too.

I identify my boundaries.
I set up my boundaries.
I establish my boundaries. I fix my boundaries.
I maintain my boundaries. I retain my boundaries.

I hide what is necessary, I hold what is important.
I act mindfully when folks are not my own.
I reveal when I need to, I conceal when I have to.
I don't trust anyone easily, I don't mistrust anyone
randomly.

I know self-protection.
I have no guilt of self-protection.
I follow self-protection.
I live in self-protection.

20. To Complete A Task

I am disciplined.
I am determined.
I am motivated.
I am strong-willed.
I am steadfast.
I am consistent.
I am persistent.

I have my plan. I make my plan.
I understand my plan.
I have necessary resources and relevant skills.
I gather information and insights as well.
I follow my plan. I set my goals.
I break it down to focus on it a little more.

I review and learn.
I rejoice and reward.

I move forward with my own helping hand.
I finish my task with an occasional rest.

21. Follow Your Intuition

I am intuitive.
I am instinctive.
I call it a gut feeling.
I name it a first thought.
I rename it as my intellect.
I know it's my innate.
I see it as my inner voice.
I think it as my calling.
I perceive it as my awakening.
I feel it as my sixth sense.

I trust my intuition for its insight.
I listen to my intuition for its foresight.
I follow my intuition for its foreknowledge.

I have a strong intuition.
I acknowledge the power of my intuition.
I act in accordance with my intuition.
I am intuition.
I am intuition.